QUIZ BOOK 3

Derek O'Brien was born in Kolkata. He began his career as a journalist for *Sportsworld* magazine but soon shifted to advertising. After working for a number of very successful years as Creative Head of Ogilvy, Derek decided to focus all his energy and talent in his passion—quizzing.

Today, Derek is Asia's best-known quizmaster and the CEO of Derek O'Brien & Associates. He is the host of the longest-running game show on Indian television, the Cadbury Bournvita Quiz Contest, for which he was voted the Best Anchor of a Game Show at the Indian Television Academy Awards for three years in a row. Always innovating, Derek is also credited with having conducted the first quiz on Twitter in 2010.

Derek has written over fifty bestselling reference, quiz and textbooks. In 2011, he was voted to the Rajya Sabha as a Member of Parliament (MP) and is the Leader of the Trinamool Congress in the Rajya Sabha.

Keep in touch with Derek on Twitter, where his handle is @quizderek.

Other books by Derek O'Brien
(published by Rupa Publications)

Bournvita Quiz Contest Quiz Book 2012

The Ultimate BQC Book of Knowledge (Volumes 1 and 2)

The Best of BQC

Derek's Challenge

Speak Up, Speak Out:
My Favourite Elocution Pieces and How to Deliver Them

My Way: Success Mantras of 12 Achievers

Derek Introduces: 100 Iconic Indians

Bournvita Quiz Contest Quiz Book 2014

QUIZ BOOK 3

DEREK O'BRIEN

Published by
Rupa Publications India Pvt. Ltd. 2015
7/16, Ansari Road, Daryaganj
New Delhi 110002

Sales centres:
Allahabad Bengaluru Chennai
Hyderabad Jaipur Kathmandu
Kolkata Mumbai

Copyright © Derek O'Brien & Associates 2015

All rights reserved.
No part of this publication may be reproduced, transmitted,
or stored in a retrieval system, in any form or by any means,
electronic, mechanical, photocopying, recording or otherwise,
without the prior permission of the publisher.

ISBN: 978-81-291-3715-9

Second impression 2016

10 9 8 7 6 5 4 3 2

Moral right of the author has been asserted.

Printed and bound in India by Repro Knowledgecast Limited, Thane

This book is sold subject to the condition that it shall not, by
way of trade or otherwise, be lent, resold, hired out, or otherwise circulated,
without the publisher's prior consent, in any form of binding or cover other than
that in which it is published.

Introduction

It is for over twenty years now that I have been interacting with students and asking questions on the sets of the iconic Bournvita Quiz Contest (BQC). The journey has been truly rewarding and enjoyable, even as I continue my work, in my much newer avatar, as a Member of Parliament in the Rajya Sabha.

The legendary quiz started off as a radio programme, in 1972, and was hosted by the late Hamid Sayani, and later by his brother Ameen.

In 1992, Cadbury (Mondelez India Foods Limited) decided to shift BQC to the more popular medium of the time—television. And thus began our journey. Over the years BQC has changed with the times. Initially an English programme, in 2011 we decided to make it a bilingual show in English and Hindi to reach a much larger audience. The growing popularity of BQC encouraged us to even launch the multi award-winning show in Tamil in 2013.

With the realisation that the future is the Internet, we decided to make a revolutionary and tectonic shift from television to the Internet. In 2014, BQC became the first example of a major offline show to go all-online in India.

To add to this, the BQC mobile app was also introduced to give the viewer a chance to play along in real time. Yes, now you can pit your brains against the top middle-school quizzers in the country!

As exciting as the online shows, are the city finals that we conduct in eighty cities across India, searching for the top schools to compete online. These quizzes are hosted by my brilliant colleagues from Derek O'Brien & Associates.

But the real heroes and torch bearers of this legendary programme for the past two decades are not us, but the principals, teachers, parents and students. Thank you ever so much for making the Bournvita Quiz Contest what it is today. It is thanks to you that BQC has endured the test of TRPs and changing times.

This book is a compilation of the best questions asked on BQC last year. It is a small tribute to all of you who have over the years watched your favourite knowledge show every week on television, and to all who watch and play along on YouTube. We are humbled by your love and hope you will enjoy this brand new addition to the BQC quiz book series.

With every good wish,
Derek O'Brien

Hall of Fame

PAST WINNERS OF THE BOURNVITA QUIZ CONTEST

1994-1995, Mumbai
Campion High School, Mumbai
Balakrishnan Sivaraman/ Sudhanshu Bhuwalka

1995-1996, Mumbai
Kendriya Vidyalaya, Powai, Mumbai
Eipy Koshy/Gourav Shah

1996-1997, Mumbai
Bombay International High School, Mumbai
Nirica Borges/Advait Behara

1997, Mumbai
Mount Saint Mary's School, New Delhi
Joe Christy/Maninder Singh Jessel

1997-1998, Mumbai
Bombay Scottish High School, Mumbai
Shaambhavi Pandyaa/ Rahul Lalmalani

1998, Mumbai
Sacred Heart Convent School, Jamshedpur

Ela Verma/ Lavanya Raghavan

1998-1999, Mumbai
Indian School Al Ghubra, Muscat
Anand Raghavan/ Hitesh Kanvatirtha

1999, Mumbai
Maneckji Cooper High School, Mumbai
Ipsita Bandopadhyay/ Gourav Bhattacharya

1999-2000, Mumbai
Chettinad Vidyashram, Chennai
Siddharth/ Karthik Das

2000-2001, Mumbai
Bharatiya Vidya Bhavan, Hyderabad
Ananya Bhaskar/ Aksha Anand

2001 September, Mumbai
Brightlands, Dehradun
Ankur Bharadwaj/ Shray Sharma

2001 December, Mumbai
Little Flower High School, Hyderabad
G Mithilesh/ K. Siddharth Reddy

2002 February, Bentota, Sri Lanka
G.D. Birla Centre For Education, Kolkata
Namrata Basu/ Rituparna Dey

2002 June, Mumbai
Kerala Samajam Public School, Jamshedpur
Saurav Biswas/Kunal Mohan

2002 September, Mumbai
Jamnabai Narsee School, Mumbai

Sharan Narayanan/ Vishnu Shrest

2003 January, Kerala
Naval Public High School, Mumbai
Apoorva Sharma/ Abhishek Pandit

2003 May, Kolkata
St. Patrick's Higher Secondary School, Asansol
Pushpen Dasgupta/ Shamik Ray

2003 October, Sangla
St. Agnes Loreto Day School, Lucknow
Aastha Srivastava/ Illa Gupta

2004 February, Swabhumi, Kolkata
Apeejay School, Jalandhar
Mohit Thukral/ Sahil Sareen

2004 May, Kenilworth, Utorda, Goa
Springdales School, Delhi
Anirudh Sridhar/ B. Anuraag

2004 July, Indian Military Academy, Dehradun
The Mother's International School, Delhi
Krittika Adhikary/ Milind Ganjoo

2004 November, Kolkata
Amity International, New Delhi
Aishwarya Singhal/ Adarsh Modi

2005 February, Kolkata
St. Kabir Ahmedabad
Yogarshi Vyas/ Helish Sharma

2005 May, Kolkata
Brightlands, Dehradun

Akshay Sharma/ Avantika Singh

2005 August, Kolkata
Amity International, New Delhi
Utkarsh Johari/ Aishwarya Singhal

2006 July, Kolkata
Riverdale High School, Dehradun
Kartikeya Panwar/ Sumit Nair

2006 November, Kolkata
Seth Jaipuria School, Lucknow
Ratnaksha Lele/ Ananya Kumar Singh

2011 August, Kolkata
Amity International School, Noida
Kripi Badonia/ Shinjini Biswas

2012 January, Kolkata
Birla Vidya Niketan, New Delhi
Anusha Malhotra/ Nitya Bansal

2013 January, Kolkata
Vidyaniketan Public School(Ullal), Bengaluru
Shashank Niranjan Gowda, Mainak Mandal

2014 December, Kolkata
Centre Point, Amravati Road, Nagpur
Ratnasambhav Sahu/Tanaya Ramani

Credits

DIRECTOR	Derek O'Brien
EXECUTIVE PRODUCERS	Nayan Chaudhury
	Sunil Shah
	Andrew Scolt
	Shalini Chaudhury
	Amit Ghosh
PRODUCER	Prabuddha Chatterjee (Gulu)
ONLINE DIRECTOR	Dongrej Gor
SENIOR RESEARCH ASSOCIATES	Anik Ghosal
	Srirupa Roy
RESEARCH ASSOCIATES	Ammar Hamid
	Ayashman Dey
	Devarshi Ghosh
	Abhishikta Bannerjee
	Arpita Sinha
	Sylvia Eugene

SENIOR RELATIONSHIP ASSOCIATES	Heena Ade (Israni)
	Sheldon Alliew
	Aubrey Whyte
	Calvin Tully
	Dipankar Rao
	Laressa Gomez
RELATIONSHIP ASSOCIATES	Durjoy Guha
	Daniel Johns
	Natasha Gasper
	Shaun Ward
	Ezekiel Mani
	Doyson Gomes
	Lyndon Gomes
	Dennis Rozario
	Ryan Price
	Agnelo Gonsalves
	Nigel Salters
	Avns Prasad
	Tunir Kumar
	Louis John
	Bhavish Gamage
	Tapan Roy
SENIOR FINANCE ASSOCIATE	Kalyanmoy Hazra
SENIOR DESIGN ASSOCIATE	Mahua Basu
SENIOR PRODUCTION ASSOCIATES	Sreevalsa Menon
	Shane Baptiste

PRODUCTION ASSOCIATES	Supriyo Nandi
	Vinu Joseph
	Victor Bhat
CREATIVE (POST)	Vivek Iyer
EDITOR	Varun Sharma
MUSIC	Shankar, Ehsaan, Loy
SOUND	Barun Kumar Chakrabarty
SET DESIGN & FABRICATION	Kosmos India
SHOT AT	Purple Movie Town
PRODUCTION ASSISTANTS	Pabitra Ghosh
	Mrinal Chakraborty
	Ananta Behera
	Indrajit Saha
	Bipin Kumar Jha
	Sudip Dey

SET 1

TAKE YOUR PICK

1. Which are the tallest of all marsupials?
   a) Kangaroos
   b) Koalas
   c) Wombats
   d) Tasmanian devils

2. The Nalanda Suite and the Marble Hall are parts of which building situated in Delhi?
   a) Red Fort
   b) Parliament House
   c) Qutb Minar
   d) Rashtrapati Bhavan

3. Which of the following would you find on the logo of the application Instagram?
   a) A hummingbird
   b) A lightning bolt
   c) A clock
   d) A camera

4. Which of these planets is not named after Greek or Roman gods and goddesses?
   a) Mars
   b) Uranus
   c) Venus
   d) Earth

5. Who was the first serving president of India to cast a vote in a general election?
   a) N. Sanjiva Reddy
   b) K.R. Narayanan
   c) Giani Zail Singh
   d) Zakir Hussain

6. If a Britisher calls it an aubergine, what do we usually call it?
   a) Cauliflower
   b) Potato
   c) Brinjal
   d) Cabbage

7. Who named more than seventy cities after himself, including one at the mouth of the Nile?
   a) Attila the Hun
   b) Napoleon
   c) Alexander the Great
   d) Julius Caesar

8. The summit of Mount Koussi in Chad is the highest point of which desert?
   a) Sahara
   b) Namib

c) Gobi
   d) Kalahari

9. What did the first postage stamp of independent India depict?
   a) Peacock
   b) Mahatma Gandhi
   c) Red Fort
   d) Tricolour

10. Which of these was introduced at the 1920 Antwerp Olympic Games?
    a) Mascot
    b) Olympic flag with five rings
    c) Torch relay
    d) Gold medals

11. The television series *Bharat Ek Khoj* was based on a book written by whom?
    a) Pandit Nehru
    b) C. Rajagopalachari
    c) Dr Rajendra Prasad
    d) Subhas Chandra Bose

12. Which key usually appears between the 'Alt' keys on a 'Qwerty' keyboard?
    a) Enter
    b) Space bar
    c) Tab
    d) Shift

13. In the human body, the primary function of which organ is to remove waste and excess water?
    a) Heart
    b) Liver
    c) Large intestine
    d) Kidney

14. Apart from C.V. Raman and A.P.J. Abdul Kalam, who was awarded the Bharat Ratna for his contribution to science?
    a) Homi Bhabha
    b) C.N.R. Rao
    c) Jagadish Chandra Bose
    d) Vikram Sarabhai

15. The word 'Pashmina' comes from the Persian word for...
    a) Silk
    b) Cotton
    c) Wool
    d) Jute

BUZZER

1. A mushroom is a fungus: serious or joking?
2. On which part of the body is a choker worn: neck or wrist?
3. For which film did Vidya Balan win the Best Actress Award at the 2013 Filmfare Awards?
4. Which colour appears between blue and yellow in the

spectrum?
5. In the acronym 'SAARC', what does 'R' stand for?
6. Which volcano in Japan last erupted in 1707?
7. In the Ramayana, who was the mother of Luv and Kusha?
8. Fill in the blank to complete the proverb: a _____ can't change its spots.
9. In the metric system, how many teaspoons make a tablespoon: two or three?
10. How many pieces are there on the board at the beginning of a game of chess?
11. Which is the highest of the three Padma awards: Shri, Bhushan or Vibhushan?
12. Babur's tomb is located in which modern-day country?

SET 2

TAKE YOUR PICK

1. Who was the first batsman to score 400 runs in each of the first seven editions of the IPL?
   a) Suresh Raina
   b) Michael Hussey
   c) M. S. Dhoni
   d) Adam Gilchrist

2. How do we popularly know the caves locally known as 'Verul Leni' in Maharashtra?
   a) Bhimbetka Rock Shelters
   b) Ellora Caves
   c) Elephanta Caves
   d) Ajanta Caves

3. What appears when a person has read a message sent by you on WhatsApp?
   a) Blue ticks
   b) Blue hearts
   c) Blue circles
   d) Blue lines

4. Almost half the total silver mined annually is used in which industry?
   a) Photography
   b) Mining
   c) Pharmaceuticals
   d) Food

5. What is the minimum age required to be a member of the Rajya Sabha?
   a) Twenty years
   b) Thirty years
   c) Forty years
   d) Fifty years

6. Which of these is served as sliced meat roasted on a spit?
   a) Falafel
   b) Shawarma
   c) Hummus
   d) Keema

7. The wings of which of these birds have been modified into flippers?
   a) Ostriches
   b) Penguins
   c) Hens
   d) Pelicans

8. Who published his first collection of poems at the age of sixteen under the pseudonym Bhanushingho, meaning 'The Sun Lion'?
   a) Pranab Mukherjee

b) Rabindranath Tagore
c) Bankim Chandra Chatterjee
d) Kazi Nazrul Islam

9. The Rupee is the currency of which of these countries?
   a) Bhutan
   b) Myanmar
   c) Afghanistan
   d) Mauritius

10. The shape of the stomach in the human body resembles which letter?
    a) C
    b) J
    c) S
    d) T

11. The Palk Strait lies between India and which other country?
    a) Bangladesh
    b) Nepal
    c) Pakistan
    d) Sri Lanka

12. Among these ranks of the Indian Police Service, which is the highest?
    a) Commissioner
    b) Sub-Inspector
    c) Inspector
    d) Superintendent

13. The first Indian postage stamp commemorating Mahatma Gandhi, issued in 1948, contained the word 'Bapu' in which two languages?
    a) Gujarati and English
    b) Hindi and Urdu
    c) English and Hindi
    d) Gujarati and Marathi

14. What kind of an animal was Richard Parker in the film *Life of Pi*?
    a) Lion
    b) Tiger
    c) Horse
    d) Camel

15. Which of the following is a textile-dyeing technique native to the island of Java?
    a) Chikankari
    b) Batik
    c) Phulkari
    d) Ikat

BUZZER

1. In India, dalchini is a form of pulse: serious or joking?
2. Which is the first month of the Gregorian calendar to have thirty-one days?
3. Which part of the face connects the muzzle of a gun and the place where a river enters the sea?
4. Which gemstone now weighs 108.93 carats, having lost

43 per cent of its original weight?
5. What is the winter capital of Jammu and Kashmir?
6. 'Aranya Kanda' and 'Kishkindha Kanda' are sections of which epic?
7. The youngest prime minister of India till date was the grandson of which prime minister?
8. *The Investigation of the State of Aether in Magnetic Fields* was the first 'scientific paper' of which physicist?
9. In which city in Pakistan is Lollywood based?
10. I am very heavy but backwards I'm not. Which word am I?
11. The rackets for which sport are covered with ordinary pimpled rubber?
12. A geographical feature rising over 1,000 feet above its surrounding area is called a mountain or valley?

SET 3

TAKE YOUR PICK

1. In India, which of these posts has never been held by a lady?
   a) The President
   b) The Vice-President
   c) The Prime Minister
   d) The Chief Minister

2. Which city is served by Chaudhary Charan Singh International Airport?
   a) Patna
   b) Dehradun
   c) Lucknow
   d) Raipur

3. Who among these was a descendant of Timur and Genghis Khan?
   a) Sher Shah
   b) Babur
   c) Tipu Sultan
   d) Iltutmish

4. In the inaugural edition of ISL, apart from Goa, which was the only other state to feature in the name of a team?
   a) Kerala
   b) Maharashtra
   c) Karnataka
   d) Gujarat

5. In 1859, who quit school and started working as a trainboy on the railroad between Detroit and Port Huron?
   a) Albert Einstein
   b) Thomas Alva Edison
   c) Alexander Graham Bell
   d) Benjamin Franklin

6. The national anthem of India was originally written in which language?
   a) Hindi
   b) English
   c) Tamil
   d) Bengali

7. Who would you consult if you were affected by 'caries'?
   a) Dermatologist
   b) Pulmonologist
   c) Dentist
   d) Hepatologist

8. The scientific name of which animal has the suffix 'unicornis'?

a) Blackbuck
   b) Indian rhinoceros
   c) Hippopotamus
   d) Musk deer

9. Which mathematical sign was introduced by Robert Recorde in 1557?
   a) Equals to
   b) Plus
   c) Minus
   d) Percentage

10. Which of these is not the title of an autobiography?
    a) *Wings of Fire*
    b) *Long Walk to Freedom*
    c) *The Diary of a Young Girl*
    d) *A Brief History of Time*

11. Which river was referred to as Zaradros by the Greeks?
    a) Chenab
    b) Ravi
    c) Beas
    d) Sutlej

12. In 2014, India regained its position as the largest consumer of gold in the world from which country?
    a) China
    b) USA
    c) Italy
    d) Germany

13. Raisins are partially dried forms of which of these?
    a) Oranges
    b) Dates
    c) Grapes
    d) Cherries

14. Which actor's screen name was Vijay in more than twenty Hindi films?
    a) Rishi Kapoor
    b) Amitabh Bachchan
    c) Dharmendra
    d) Hrithik Roshan

15. Which function key activates the 'Help' menu on a standard computer keyboard?
    a) F4
    b) F3
    c) F2
    d) F1

BUZZER

1. Oysters are not the only type of molluscs that can produce pearls: serious or joking?
2. In which series of films would you meet a vampire named Edward Cullen?
3. Whose portrait appeared on the first stamp in the world, the Penny Black?
4. What weighs more: a kilogram of iron or a kilogram of feathers?

5. In the Gregorian calendar, which is the first month to have exactly thirty days?
6. In fiction, who employed the Baker Street Irregulars as informers?
7. Guru Peak in Mount Abu is the highest peak of which mountain range?
8. In 1924, which statue was designated as a National Monument in the United States of America?
9. In Indian Railways, what does the class code 'SL' stand for?
10. Who was sworn in as prime minister for a second term on 22 May 2009?
11. Which is the only planet of the solar system whose name ends with a vowel?
12. Which country does Rafael Nadal represent in tennis?

SET 4

TAKE YOUR PICK

1. In Twitter, what do the letters 'RT' stand for?
   a) Real Tweet
   b) Run Time
   c) Retweet
   d) Repeat Tweet

2. Which of these animals has two hair-covered horns called ossicones?
   a) Camel
   b) Giraffe
   c) Kangaroo
   d) Blackbuck

3. Travelling from north to south, which of the following places will you reach last?
   a) Patna
   b) Darjeeling
   c) Panaji
   d) Nagpur

4. Which of these food items shares its name with a famous lane in Delhi?
   a) Paratha
   b) Tandoori
   c) Paneer
   d) Rezala

5. Which was the first foreign country to issue postage stamps with Gandhiji's picture?
   a) South Africa
   b) The United States of America
   c) The United Kingdom
   d) France

6. Which of these is not a card shown during a hockey match?
   a) Red card
   b) Green card
   c) Yellow card
   d) Blue card

7. *On the Nature of Reality* documents were conversations between Rabindranath Tagore and which other person?
   a) Thomas Edison
   b) Albert Einstein
   c) Alfred Nobel
   d) C.V. Raman

8. Which leader's father was a senior economist for the Government of Kenya?
   a) Angela Merkel

b) Sheikh Hasina
c) Barack Obama
d) Aung San Suu Kyi

9. Which of these characters was not created by Agatha Christie?
   a) Thomas Beresford
   b) Perry Mason
   c) Parker Pyne
   d) Hercule Poirot

10. What is the minimum age you need to be to get an Indian passport?
    a) Fifteen years
    b) Eighteen years
    c) Twenty-one years
    d) None

11. The jejunum and the ileum are parts of what in the human body?
    a) Stomach
    b) Liver
    c) Small intestine
    d) Large intestine

12. If Shah Jahan built the Taj Mahal, what did Hamida Banu Begum build?
    a) Gol Gumbaz
    b) Diwan-i-Khas
    c) Victoria Memorial
    d) Humayun's Tomb

13. More than 70 km long, what is sometimes referred to as the 'white snake'?
    a) The Ganges
    b) Khyber Pass
    c) The Siachen Glacier
    d) Nilgiri mountains

14. Bond, book, Bristol and kraft are some of the important grades of which everyday item?
    a) Pencil
    b) Paper
    c) Eraser
    d) Pen

15. What is the official religion of Cambodia?
    a) Buddhism
    b) Sikhism
    c) Jainism
    d) Zoroastrianism

BUZZER

1. Param Vir Chakra may be given posthumously: serious or joking?
2. Kohl is usually used as make-up for which part of the body?
3. The cartoon character Doraemon originated in which country?
4. Which grain is the staple food of about half of the world's population?

5. The name of which 'life-saving' object means 'protection against fall' in French?
6. Which road in India was called the 'Long Walk' by European travellers?
7. Which book was written by R.L. Stevenson: *Treasure Island* or *Gulliver's Travels*?
8. Which Indian president was immediately succeeded by the first woman president?
9. With which vegetable would you associate a person who takes little or no exercise?
10. Rearrange the letters of the words PEN and TUNE to get the name of a planet.
11. The highest altitude zoological garden in India is located in which state of India?
12. In cricket, the Border–Gavaskar Trophy is played between India and…?

SET 5

TAKE YOUR PICK

1. In India, Sansarpur has produced some of the most famous players in which sport?
   a) Hockey
   b) Cricket
   c) Kho kho
   d) Kabaddi

2. Which of these is the largest predatory fish in the world?
   a) Dolphin
   b) Blue whale
   c) Great white shark
   d) Swordfish

3. With which of these applications is the phrase 'Last seen' most commonly associated?
   a) YouTube
   b) WhatsApp
   c) Instagram
   d) Twitter

4. Which of these products is obtained from plants?
   a) Honey
   b) Silk
   c) Rubber
   d) Lac

5. Which Lok Sabha constituency in India has the least number of voters?
   a) Lakshadweep
   b) Daman and Diu
   c) Puducherry
   d) South Goa

6. Raudri, Ravani, and Sarasvati are the ancient names of which musical instrument?
   a) Veena
   b) Tabla
   c) Harmonium
   d) Flute

7. Who among these was not a part of the conspiracy to assassinate Julius Caesar?
   a) Cassius
   b) Mark Antony
   c) Brutus
   d) Casca

8. In the human body, the size of what increases in proportion to the difficulty of a task?
   a) Finger nails
   b) Pupils
   c) Hair

d) Teeth

9. The Rashtrapati Bhavan in Delhi was the erstwhile residence of the British...
   a) Governor-General
   b) Viceroy
   c) Prime Minister
   d) Queen

10. Which river in India is often referred to as the 'Vridha Ganga' because of its length?
    a) Godavari
    b) Cauvery
    c) Krishna
    d) Luni

11. Which feat connects James Irwin, David Scott and Alan Shepard?
    a) Climbing Mt Everest
    b) Landing on the moon
    c) Reaching North Pole
    d) Discovering Antarctica

12. Ib in Odisha and Od in Gujarat are...
    a) Shortest names of railway stations
    b) Smallest towns in India
    c) Largest towns in India
    d) Largest ports in India

13. Which word connects the cooking of an egg and an illegal action?
    a) Boil

b) Skillet
   c) Poach
   d) Scramble

14. Which punctuation mark forms a part of the logo of 'Incredible India'?
    a) Full stop
    b) Exclamation mark
    c) Semi colon
    d) Question mark

15. Generally, Warli paintings are painted on a mud base using one colour, which is…
    a) White
    b) Blue
    c) Green
    d) Orange

BUZZER

1. Albert Einstein was the first man to televise pictures of objects in motion: serious or joking?
2. Which phrase, also the name of a film, means 'I have cut the kite', in Gujarati?
3. The name of which egg preparation comes from a French word meaning 'knife blade'?
4. Bob, bun and crew are different styles of shoes or hairstyles?
5. '.hk' is the Internet country code for which special administrative region of China?

6. The term 'smog' comes from 'fog' and which other word?
7. Which empire in India came earlier: the Guptas or the Mauryas?
8. In which state is the Mamallapuram Dance Festival held?
9. Which is a type of embroidery: chikankari or bidri?
10. In which language was the Rigveda composed?
11. Which footballer was awarded the FIFA Ballon D'Or for 2014?
12. Which is the only continent where bees are not found?

SET 6

TAKE YOUR PICK

1. Which was the most visited ticketed monument in 2014?
   a) The Taj Mahal
   b) The Eiffel Tower
   c) The Statue of Liberty
   d) The Leaning Tower of Pisa

2. In 2013, 90 per cent of all malaria deaths in the world occurred in which continent?
   a) Asia
   b) Africa
   c) North America
   d) Europe

3. Fire, pharaoh, army and carpenter are different types of...
   a) Spiders
   b) Cockroaches
   c) Ants
   d) Bees

4. Who acts as president of India when the offices of both President and vice-president fall vacant?
   a) Chief of Army Staff
   b) Chief Justice of India
   c) Speaker of Lok Sabha
   d) Attorney General

5. Which language is also known in some areas as 'Gorkha Bhasa'?
   a) Konkani
   b) Nepali
   c) Manipuri
   d) Maithili

6. What did the first webcam in the world show?
   a) Coffee pot
   b) Computer
   c) Traffic jam
   d) Apple

7. Which word comes from the Sanskrit words meaning 'bowing action'?
   a) Swagatam
   b) Shukriya
   c) Alvida
   d) Namaskar

8. At 77,700 square km, which state has the largest forest cover in India?
   a) Kerala
   b) Madhya Pradesh
   c) Tamil Nadu

d) Uttar Pradesh

9. In the human body, ball and socket, and hinge are types of...
   a) Fats
   b) Muscles
   c) Joints
   d) Cells

10. Who among these was not a Navratna in Akbar's court?
    a) Todar Mal
    b) Abul Fazl
    c) Faizi
    d) Bairam Khan

11. Which of these capital cities is situated in Asia?
    a) Cairo
    b) Jakarta
    c) Lima
    d) Amsterdam

12. Which profession would you be in if you wore a toque?
    a) Doctor
    b) Lawyer
    c) Chef
    d) Policeman

13. Who among these was the fastest to score 6,000 ODI runs?
    a) Rohit Sharma

b) Suresh Raina
   c) Virat Kohli
   d) M.S. Dhoni

14. What is the colour of the circle on the symbol for vegetarian food on food packets?
    a) Brown
    b) White
    c) Green
    d) Blue

15. Phulkari, meaning 'flower work', is a form of which of these?
    a) Embroidery
    b) Sculpting
    c) Paper folding
    d) Flower arranging

BUZZER

1. Qutb-ud-Din Aibak built only the first storey of the Qutb Minar: serious or joking?
2. With which author would you associate the characters Cheshire Cat and Mad Hatter?
3. The name of which art form of India comes from the Sanskrit words for 'canvas' and 'picture'?
4. Which of these honours Indian cinema: Jnanpith Award or Dadasaheb Phalke Award?
5. The name of which part of an egg means yellow?
6. What, used in everyday life, gets wet when used for drying?

7. Which is the odd one out: heptagon, triangle, rectangle, cube, pentagon?
8. The southernmost tip of which union territory is only 150 km away from Sumatra, Indonesia?
9. Which festival is known as Fagu in Nepal?
10. Ne is the symbol of which chemical element?
11. Who, along with his daughter Sonia Sanwalka, wrote his autobiography *The Race of My Life*?
12. Which of these are found near the Arctic Circle: penguins or polar bears?

SET 7

TAKE YOUR PICK

1. Prickly heat is associated with which part of the human body?
   a) Hair
   b) Skin
   c) Tongue
   d) Nails

2. Which of these big cats cannot roar?
   a) Lion
   b) Cheetah
   c) Jaguar
   d) Tiger

3. Gandhiji wrote that we must learn to live and die like Socrates and referred to him as a great…
   a) Swadeshi
   b) Sangrami
   c) Satyagrahi
   d) Sadhu

4. Which team has played the most IPL finals?
   a) Chennai Super Kings
   b) Mumbai Indians
   c) Kolkata Knight Riders
   d) Kings XI Punjab

5. In Facebook, you have the option of changing your language to which of these?
   a) English (Mafia)
   b) English (Daredevil)
   c) English (Pirate)
   d) English (Hoodlum)

6. According to Albert Einstein, '____ is more important than knowledge.' Fill in the blank.
   a) Education
   b) Learning
   c) Imagination
   d) Intelligence

7. In which of these artforms are characters grouped as pacha, kathi and thadi?
   a) Kathak
   b) Bharatanatyam
   c) Kuchipudi
   d) Kathakali

8. G.V. Mavalankar, N. Sanjiva Reddy and P.A. Sangma all held which post in India?
   a) Chairman, Rajya Sabha
   b) Chairman, Planning Commission
   c) Speaker, Lok Sabha

d) Governor, RBI

9. The name of which legendary prince of Denmark, a hero in a Shakespearean play, also means a small village?
   a) Romeo
   b) Hamlet
   c) Macbeth
   d) Henry

10. In 2013, which Indian institution was awarded the dedicated pin code '110201'?
    a) Parliament House
    b) Supreme Court
    c) Gateway of India
    d) Rashtrapati Bhavan

11. Rajaraja I, the builder of the Brihadishvara Temple at Tanjore, belonged to which dynasty?
    a) Chera
    b) Chola
    c) Pandya
    d) Maurya

12. Which of these countries shares the shortest international boundary with India?
    a) Nepal
    b) China
    c) Myanmar
    d) Bhutan

13. In India, the number 102 is traditionally reserved for calling which of these?
    a) Police
    b) Ambulance
    c) Fire brigade
    d) None of the above

14. Which of these varieties of mangoes is named after a Portuguese general?
    a) Alphonso
    b) Banganapalli
    c) Himsagar
    d) Chausa

15. On a standard keyboard, what is pressed along with 'Delete' to remove files permanently?
    a) Shift
    b) Alt
    c) Space bar
    d) Enter

BUZZER

1. Tanjore paintings originated in Tamil Nadu: serious or joking?
2. Who played the role of Haider in the 2014 film of the same name?
3. At the Olympics, Dressage, Eventing and Jumping involve which animal?
4. What is the main ingredient of the dish 'upma'?

5. The Doberman originated in which country?
6. Which celestial body appears on the flag of China?
7. In which category did Winston Churchill win the Nobel Prize in 1953?
8. Which group of caves is situated 100 km north-east of Ellora?
9. In India, to whose empire did Seleucus I send Megasthenes?
10. In India, Beating the Retreat marks the end of the Republic Day celebrations or Independence Day celebrations?
11. How many lines does a sonnet consist of?
12. The name of what comes from the Greek word for 'holding first place': protein or carbohydrate?

SET 8

TAKE YOUR PICK

1. What did the Royal Bengal tiger replace as the national animal of India?
   a) One-horned rhinoceros
   b) Elephant
   c) Asiatic lion
   d) Indian spotted deer

2. If you are travelling on Indian Railways with the ticket code 'CC', then you are travelling in…
   a) AC 2 Tier
   b) AC Chair Car
   c) First Class
   d) Sleeper Class

3. In which sport did India win a medal for the first time ever at the 2012 London Olympic Games?
   a) Wrestling
   b) Hockey
   c) Shooting
   d) Badminton

4. Which of these gases is commonly used to disinfect water and is part of the sanitation process for sewage and industrial waste?
   a) Ammonia
   b) Hydrogen
   c) Chlorine
   d) Helium

5. Who was the first Indian president to visit the world's highest battlefield, the Siachen Glacier?
   a) Pratibha Patil
   b) A.P.J. Abdul Kalam
   c) Pranab Mukherjee
   d) No one has

6. On which contemporary currency note of India would you see the image of a satellite?
   a) Rs 100
   b) Rs 500
   c) Rs 1,000
   d) No note

7. Which is the most common reason for getting bilirubin levels tested?
   a) Jaundice
   b) Conjunctivitis
   c) Malaria
   d) Measles

8. The tomb of which of these rulers is not situated in Delhi?
   a) Firoz Shah Tughlaq

b) Sikander Lodi
   c) Humayun
   d) Tipu Sultan

9. Which continent is classified as a desert?
   a) Asia
   b) Antarctica
   c) Europe
   d) North America

10. Which term is derived from a Greek word meaning 'number'?
    a) Astronomy
    b) Arithmetic
    c) Mensuration
    d) Algebra

11. Pencil, toothbrush and handlebar are different types of what?
    a) Skirts
    b) Moustaches
    c) Heels
    d) Hairstyles

12. Which of these fruits is also known as Indian gooseberry?
    a) Angoor
    b) Amrood
    c) Amla
    d) Anar

13. While using Windows, if you press the Control and

Escape keys together, what will happen?
a) Program shuts down
b) Start Menu opens
c) Open documents are deleted permanently
d) Screen gets locked

14. Traditionally, the white colour used in Madhubani paintings is obtained from...
    a) Milk
    b) Curd
    c) Rice
    d) Paneer

15. Spread, button-down, forward point and club are some of the types of what?
    a) Collars
    b) Skirts
    c) Shoes
    d) Sleeves

BUZZER

1. Apples can also be green in colour: serious or joking?
2. '.in' is the Internet code of which country?
3. Who has the Omnitrix, a watch-shaped device?
4. Alphabetically, the name of which month would come just after July?
5. Which country is home to eight of the world's ten highest peaks?
6. In which Indian state are the majority of Asiatic lions

found?
7. The Battle of Waterloo ended whose brief second reign?
8. Which is the odd one out: femur, mandible, fibula, tibia, patella?
9. In which state is the Nashik Kumbh Mela held?
10. The word 'lunatic' comes from the Latin word for which heavenly body?
11. Which word connects a person who observes and the screen of a computer?
12. Which hockey player's birthday is celebrated as National Sports Day in India?

SET 9

TAKE YOUR PICK

1. How many digits are there in the Aadhar number issued by 'UIDAI'?
   a) Twelve
   b) Fourteen
   c) Sixteen
   d) Eighteen

2. Deccani, Chummarti and Sikang are Indian breeds of which animal?
   a) Horse
   b) Dog
   c) Cat
   d) Lion

3. The fuse wire used for household electricity must be made of a metal having...
   a) Low boiling point
   b) Low melting point
   c) High melting point
   d) High boiling point

4. Which north Indian city is the birthplace of three Indian Prime Ministers?
   a) Allahabad
   b) Jammu
   c) Jaipur
   d) Bhatinda

5. In which part of the human body would you find calf muscles?
   a) Cheeks
   b) Legs
   c) Abdomen
   d) Fingers

6. Deepika Kumari, Bombayla Devi Laishram and Laxmirani Majhi play which sport?
   a) Archery
   b) Badminton
   c) Volleyball
   d) Swimming

7. Garuda (a mythical half-man, half-bird figure) and the elephant, are the national symbols of which of these countries?
   a) Japan
   b) Thailand
   c) Pakistan
   d) Bangladesh

8. Nelson Mandela said, '_____ is the most powerful weapon which you can use to change the world.' Fill in the blank.

a) Imagination
b) Perseverance
c) Education
d) Action

9. The Kathiawar Peninsula is a part of which state in India?
   a) Tamil Nadu
   b) Kerala
   c) Gujarat
   d) Madhya Pradesh

10. Which of these values is equal to 10 lakh?
    a) 1 million
    b) 10 million
    c) 100 million
    d) 1 billion

11. Bharat Ratna 1990; Nobel Peace Prize 1993; Gandhi Peace Prize 2000; who are we referring to?
    a) Dalai Lama
    b) Nelson Mandela
    c) Mother Teresa
    d) Aung San Suu Kyi

12. Which of these vegetables is also known as gumbo, okra or okuru?
    a) Ladies' finger
    b) Tomato
    c) Gourd
    d) Onion

13. Shata-tantri veena or the veena with a hundred strings was the original name of which musical instrument?
    a) Mridangam
    b) Santoor
    c) Jal Tarang
    d) Sitar

14. The muslin handkerchief given by Nur Jehan to Jahangir is said to have popularised what?
    a) Zardozi
    b) Chikankari
    c) Batik
    d) Applique

15. Which of these countries follows the same time as the Indian Standard Time?
    a) Sri Lanka
    b) Nepal
    c) Bangladesh
    d) Bhutan

BUZZER

1. The Spanish word for tortoise is galápago: serious or joking?
2. The backspace key on a standard keyboard deletes characters on which side of the blinking cursor?
3. Which actor played the role of Nandu in the 2014 film *Happy New Year*?
4. Ristretto, Macchiato and Americano are types of which beverage?

5. Rearrange the letters of the word 'trance' to get a word denoting a secretion from flowers.
6. If you were visiting the Sun Temple at Konark, which state would you be in?
7. Bahadur Shah Zafar was an emperor of which dynasty?
8. The rate at which we breathe is controlled by the brain or the heart?
9. Which epic is referred to in the Adi Kavya or the First Epic?
10. In 105 AD, what was produced by Lun Tsai in China by mixing mulberry bark, hemp and rags with water?
11. Which metal was called platina del Pinto by the Spaniards for its resemblance to silver?
12. Golf player Vijay Singh belongs to which country: Fiji or India?

SET 10

TAKE YOUR PICK

1. Which of these scientific units is not named after a person?
   a) Hertz
   b) Pascal
   c) Candela
   d) Watt

2. The famous Kaziranga National Park harbours the world's largest population of which animal?
   a) Asiatic Lion
   b) Indian Rhinoceros
   c) Nilgai
   d) Gharial

3. After which feature of the Indian landscape are most trains named?
   a) Rivers
   b) Mountains
   c) Valleys
   d) Waterfalls

4. Which of these sportspersons has not had a biopic based on him/her?
   a) M.C. Mary Kom
   b) Milkha Singh
   c) Sania Mirza
   d) Paan Singh Tomar

5. Which Indian prime minister was born in Mughalsarai in Uttar Pradesh?
   a) Lal Bahadur Shastri
   b) Morarji Desai
   c) Indira Gandhi
   d) Rajiv Gandhi

6. What in India should be made of handspun and hand woven khadi?
   a) Currency note
   b) National flag
   c) Nehru Jacket
   d) Gandhi Cap

7. Which of these is the largest single cell found on Earth?
   a) The thighbone
   b) A carbon atom
   c) An elephant tusk
   d) An ostrich egg

8. Rani-Ki-Vav, meaning 'The Queen's Stepwell', was recently inducted as a UNESCO World Heritage Site. It is in which state of India?
   a) Gujarat

b) Madhya Pradesh
c) Maharashtra
d) Rajasthan

9. How many sides does a triskaidecagon have?
    a) Three
    b) Thirteen
    c) Seventeen
    d) Thirty

10. Which is the smallest country in Asia in terms of size?
    a) Sri Lanka
    b) Bangladesh
    c) Singapore
    d) Maldives

11. In 1839, Robert Cornelius, an amateur chemist, is believed to be credited with the world's first...
    a) Instant message
    b) Tweet
    c) Selfie
    d) Blog

12. Which spice is called 'cilantro' in Spanish?
    a) Coriander
    b) Cardamom
    c) Clove
    d) Pepper

13. Acoustic and Electric are two forms of which musical instrument?
    a) Tabla

b) Harmonium
c) Guitar
d) Piano

14. What connects Gharchola and Paithani?
    a) Bags
    b) Sarees
    c) Bangles
    d) Shoes

15. The original name of the road more popularly known as Marine Drive in Mumbai is named after which freedom fighter?
    a) Vallabhbhai Patel
    b) Jawaharlal Nehru
    c) Mahatma Gandhi
    d) Netaji Subhas Chandra Bose

BUZZER

1. The Nobel Prize in Literature has never been shared by two people: serious or joking?
2. Which letter immediately follows 'Y' on a 'Qwerty' keyboard?
3. Norah Jones is the daughter of which musician?
4. Which actress played the role of Rani in the 2014 film *Queen*?
5. Which state is famous for the dish litti-chokha: Maharashtra or Bihar?
6. Alphabetically, the name of which colour of the

rainbow would appear first in a dictionary?
7. Which was the first planned city of the Mughals?
8. Rearrange the letters of the words 'art' and 'sun' to get the name of a planet.
9. In the fairy tale *The Ugly Duckling*, what bird does the duckling transform into?
10. Ozone is formed from which gas?
11. For which team did Sachin Tendulkar play in the 2013 edition of the IPL?
12. The two horns of the black rhinoceros are made entirely of hardened: enamel or hair?

SET 11

TAKE YOUR PICK

1. Which of these animals can spend up to nineteen hours a day eating?
   a) Royal Bengal Tiger
   b) Indian elephant
   c) Asiatic lion
   d) Olive Ridley turtle

2. In 1575 AD, which city in Uttar Pradesh was founded by Emperor Akbar, under the name of Illahabas?
   a) Fatehpur Sikri
   b) Agra
   c) Allahabad
   d) Lucknow

3. In terms of number of days, what is the maximum duration of the Olympic Games?
   a) Sixteen
   b) Eighteen
   c) Twenty
   d) Twenty-one

4. Which of these takes the most time to break down?
   a) Paper napkin
   b) Tin can
   c) Glass bottle
   d) Nylon fabric

5. *Ficus religiosa* is the scientific name of which tree?
   a) Mango tree
   b) Neem tree
   c) Banyan tree
   d) Peepal tree

6. Dhanteras marks the beginning of which festival?
   a) Holi
   b) Diwali
   c) Guru Poornima
   d) Ganesh Chaturthi

7. Which vitamin is required by the human body to heal wounds and repair cartilage, bones and teeth?
   a) Vitamin A
   b) Vitamin B
   c) Vitamin C
   d) Vitamin D

8. The idea for which monument was proposed by Edouard de Laboulaye?
   a) The Statue of Liberty
   b) The Eiffel Tower
   c) The Sydney Opera House
   d) The Golden Gate Bridge

9. French Guiana, an overseas region of France, is located in which continent?
   a) South America
   b) Europe
   c) Asia
   d) Africa

10. Which of these can be used to remove ink stains from coloured clothes?
    a) Coconut water
    b) Mustard oil
    c) Honey
    d) Milk

11. Accidentally invented by Thomas Sullivan, what have 2,000 perforations or small holes?
    a) Mosquito nets
    b) Tea bags
    c) Postage stamps
    d) Beehives

12. The archaeological evidence of which dance form, dating back to the second century BC, is found in the caves of Udayagiri and Khandagiri near Bhubaneswar?
    a) Manipuri
    b) Kathak
    c) Odissi
    d) Kathak

13. Which of these is a long coat worn by men in India?
    a) Pheta

b) Jodhpurs
   c) Garara
   d) Achkan

14. What was the name of Robinson Crusoe's servant?
    a) Monday
    b) Wednesday
    c) Friday
    d) Saturday

15. What, apart from white, is the official colour of Canada?
    a) Yellow
    b) Red
    c) Orange
    d) Blue

BUZZER

1. Sushi and pizza originated in the same country: serious or joking?
2. What is the name of the panda in the film *Kung Fu Panda*?
3. The name of which insect comes from the Old French word meaning 'to crackle'?
4. Which word was originally used as the telegraphic address of the International Criminal Police Commission?
5. Which landmark is located in Mumbai: Gateway of India or India Gate?

6. What in the human body consists of a crown and one or more roots?
7. With which baked food item can you relate small files which are stored on a user's computer?
8. Vinayaka Chaturthi observes the birth of which Hindu deity?
9. Which word connects a substance used for sticking objects together and a part of our mouth?
10. The name of which element comes from a Greek word meaning 'something new'?
11. Which martial art, apart from Judo, is included in the Olympic Games?
12. Which state is known as 'Srigandhada Nadu', meaning the Sandalwood State?

SET 12

TAKE YOUR PICK

1. Which of these shares its name with a bone in the human body?
   a) Diameter
   b) Radius
   c) Hypotenuse
   d) Perimeter

2. Beside which monument would you find the famous Quwwat-ul-Islam Mosque?
   a) Buland Darwaza
   b) Qutb Minar
   c) Humayun's Tomb
   d) Charminar

3. The trophy for which of these does not include a bow and arrow?
   a) Dronacharya Award
   b) Eklavya Award
   c) Arjuna Award
   d) Dhyan Chand Award

4. The Aztecs gave a name meaning 'bitter water' to it and they mixed vanilla and chillies to it for flavour. What is it?
   a) Coffee
   b) Chocolate
   c) Tea
   d) Potato

5. Which is the farthest planet from Earth that can be observed by the unaided human eye?
   a) Jupiter
   b) Saturn
   c) Neptune
   d) Mars

6. If Green Revolution: Food Grains, then Round Revolution:?
   a) Eggs
   b) Tomatoes
   c) Potatoes
   d) Oranges

7. One of the distinguishing features that separates a monkey from an ape is that, most monkeys...
   a) Have whiskers
   b) Have tails
   c) Are brown
   d) Move fast

8. According to the national calendar of India, the first day of a year in a non-leap year coincides with...
   a) 1 January

b) 22 March
   c) 15 April
   d) 29 February

9. Complete the name of the Mughal emperor born in 1592: Shahab-ud-din Muhammad _____.
   a) Humayun
   b) Akbar
   c) Jehangir
   d) Shah Jahan

10. Which of these national parks is located in India?
    a) The Corbett National Park
    b) The Sagarmatha National Park
    c) The Yellowstone National Park
    d) The Serengeti National Park

11. Which country has changed its national flag the most number of times in the twentieth century?
    a) Afghanistan
    b) Sri Lanka
    c) Nepal
    d) USA

12. Which of these items of clothing is not named after an island?
    a) Capris
    b) Bermudas
    c) Cargos
    d) Hawaiian shirts

13. Which Indian union territory has around 572 islands

of which only thirty-seven are inhabited?
a) Daman and Diu
b) Lakshadweep
c) Dadra and Nagar Haveli
d) Andaman and Nicobar Islands

14. The tomato was introduced to Europe by the...
    a) Germans
    b) Spanish
    c) French
    d) Greeks

15. Who was the director of the 2014 film *PK*?
    a) Aamir Khan
    b) Rajkumar Hirani
    c) Prabhu Deva
    d) Dibakar Banerjee

BUZZER

1. Bats that feed entirely on blood are called Dracula bats: serious or joking?
2. In computers, if '.net' stands for 'network', what does '.org' stand for?
3. Which cartoon duck wears the middy blouse of a sailor suit and a sailor's hat?
4. Which spice is called zafran in Arabic?
5. Which award was created earlier: Nobel Prize or the Ramon Magsaysay Award?
6. How is the tomb of Arjumand Bano Begum better known?

7. Which organ of the human body consists of the outer epidermis and the inner dermis?
8. Which epic was born when Vyasa told Ganesh to write only after grasping the meaning?
9. Which colour is common to the flags of China, Nepal and Canada?
10. A greater percentage of the Sundarbans mangrove forest lies in India or Bangladesh?
11. Which state celebrates its formation day as Utkal Divas on 1 April?
12. In Indian Badminton League, the team Awadhe Warriors is based in which city?

SET 13

TAKE YOUR PICK

1. Which breed of dog can run the fastest?
   a) Afghan hound
   b) Greyhound
   c) Doberman
   d) Basset hound

2. Which building, designed by British architect Edwin Lutyens, is located at Raisina Hill in New Delhi?
   a) Lotus Temple
   b) Teen Murti Bhavan
   c) Rashtrapati Bhavan
   d) India Gate

3. Which of these is not included in the Olympic triathlon?
   a) Swimming
   b) Running
   c) Cycling
   d) Shooting

4. Clementine and Tangerine are varieties of which citrus fruit?
   a) Apple
   b) Orange
   c) Guava
   d) Banana

5. Which of these reflects the most sunlight?
   a) Green forests
   b) Sand desert
   c) Land covered with snow
   d) Oceans

6. The name of which historical movement in India literally means 'land gift'?
   a) Appiko
   b) Bhoodan
   c) Chipko
   d) Navdanya

7. In India, nearly 90 per cent of which of these are located in rural areas?
   a) Headquarters of Indian Railways
   b) Banks
   c) Post Offices
   d) High Courts

8. What do we do about 28,000 times per day without being aware of it?
   a) Scratch
   b) Dream
   c) Blink

d) Perspire/Sweat

9. On the advice of who among these was a health commission appointed for the British army in India in the 1850s?
   a) Mother Teresa
   b) Florence Nightingale
   c) Nelson Mandela
   d) Sister Nivedita

10. The Indus river enters India through which state?
    a) Punjab
    b) Uttarakhand
    c) Jammu and Kashmir
    d) Rajasthan

11. The Sant Kabir Awards are conferred in India upon members of which profession?
    a) Fishermen
    b) Poets
    c) Singers
    d) Weavers

12. Who is the CEO of Wayne Enterprises?
    a) Spider-Man
    b) Batman
    c) Captain America
    d) Superman

13. The name of which gemstone comes from a Greek word meaning 'invincible'?
    a) Pearl

b) Ruby
c) Diamond
d) Sapphire

14. Platform, Pointe, Oxford and Mary Jane are different types of…
    a) Shoes
    b) Bags
    c) Bracelets
    d) Trousers

15. In which novel would you meet characters named Jim Hawkins and Billy Bones?
    a) *Oliver Twist*
    b) *Treasure Island*
    c) *Robinson Crusoe*
    d) *Ivanhoe*

BUZZER

1. Enamel is not living and contains no nerves: serious or joking?
2. In digital media, what is blog an abbreviation of?
3. What is the name of Chhota Bheem's pet monkey?
4. Which fruit, also known as Chinese gooseberry, is named after a bird from New Zealand?
5. In 1968, the Sveriges Riksbank, Sweden's central bank, established which award?
6. In which state are the Ajanta Caves located?
7. In the *Mahabharata*, how many Pandavas were there?

8. On whose death did Barack Obama tweet, 'Thank you, for showing us the power of one small step'?
9. Who is the only Indian cricketer to have received the Bharat Ratna?
10. What was first rolled out in Kolkata on 24 February 1873?
11. Which animal, apart from emu, holds the shield on the Australian coat of arms?
12. In *Hamlet*, what was the name of Polonius's daughter?

SET 14

TAKE YOUR PICK

1. Guy de Maupassant ridiculed which structure as a 'high and skinny pyramid of iron ladders'?
   a) The Statue of Liberty
   b) The Leaning Tower of Pisa
   c) The Eiffel Tower
   d) The Sphinx

2. What is the 'shot' in the Olympic sport shot put?
   a) Hammer
   b) Javelin
   c) Metal ring
   d) Metal ball

3. On Google, who was the most searched male actor from Bollywood in 2014?
   a) Shah Rukh Khan
   b) Ranbir Kapoor
   c) Akshay Kumar
   d) Salman Khan

4. Which of these words comes from two Greek words meaning 'beside' and 'food'?
   a) Virus
   b) Bacteria
   c) Parasite
   d) Protein

5. Which part of the human body secretes hydrochloric acid to kill the bacteria in food?
   a) Liver
   b) Stomach
   c) Small Intestine
   d) Pancreas

6. In 1915, who received the Kaiser-i-Hind Gold Medal from the British for his contribution to Ambulance services in South Africa?
   a) Subhas Chandra Bose
   b) Jawaharlal Nehru
   c) Mahatma Gandhi
   d) Vallabhbhai Patel

7. Which is the only bird to have just two toes on each foot?
   a) Penguin
   b) Emu
   c) Ostrich
   d) Kiwi

8. What in the desert is classified as crescentic, star, linear, dome and parabolic?
   a) Cacti

b) Mirages
c) Dunes
d) Oases

9. Which of these was named the 'US Word of the Year' by Oxford English Dictionary in 2009?
   a) Unfriend
   b) Tweet
   c) Selfie
   d) Phablet

10. Which of these is an Indian word for one hundred lakhs?
    a) Crore
    b) Million
    c) Kosh
    d) Rati

11. Which cell phone game includes characters like Scarlett Fox and Montana Smith?
    a) Candy Crush Saga
    b) Temple Run
    c) Subway Surfer
    d) Fruit Ninja

12. What is the colour of a komodo dragon's tongue?
    a) Red
    b) Yellow
    c) Green
    d) Blue

13. Which type of saree uses the Tie and Dye process?

a) Benarasi
b) Paithani
c) Bandhni
d) Jamdani

14. In which novel would you meet Winston Smith who works in the Ministry of Truth and alters historical records to fit the needs of the Party?
    a) *The Prince*
    b) *1984*
    c) *Gulliver's Travels*
    d) *Ivanhoe*

15. Arches, whorls, simple loops and double loops are patterns of...
    a) Leaves
    b) Fingerprints
    c) Sand dunes
    d) Corals

BUZZER

1. Bombay Duck is a variety of duck: serious or joking?
2. Which word connects the name of Chacha Chaudhary's dog and a projectile?
3. What in China begins at Shanhaiguan and ends at Jiayuguan?
4. Which is the only vowel that appears in the names of all the days of the week?
5. Which city in Haryana was the site of three battles,

fought in 1526, 1556 and 1761?
6. The right side of the heart collects oxygen-poor blood and pumps it to which organ?
7. In the *Ramayana*, what kind of creatures were Bali and Sugriva?
8. My mother's mother's only daughter is my…?
9. 'Djoker' is the nickname of which contemporary tennis ace?
10. In Indian Railways, what does the 'C' in 'RAC' stand for?
11. 'A Mad Tea-Party' and 'The Lobster Quadrille' are the chapters of which book?
12. On which colour band does the chakra on the national flag of India appear?

SET 15

TAKE YOUR PICK

1. What is a unit of information equal to 1,048,576 bytes called?
   a) Gigabyte
   b) Megabyte
   c) Terabyte
   d) Kilobyte

2. Which animal has the longest tail of all land mammals?
   a) Kangaroo
   b) Giraffe
   c) Elephant
   d) Zebra

3. Who played the role of Milkha Singh in the film *Bhaag Milkha Bhaag*?
   a) Ranbir Kapoor
   b) Farhan Akhtar
   c) Hrithik Roshan
   d) Arjun Kapoor

4. Which metal has the highest known electrical and thermal conductivity among all metals?
   a) Gold
   b) Silver
   c) Platinum
   d) Aluminium

5. Which Hindu deity is also known as Gangadhara, Chandrasekhara and Trilochana?
   a) Vishnu
   b) Shiva
   c) Krishna
   d) Brahma

6. Log, yearner, soldier, freefall and starfish are all types of what?
   a) Fictional warriors
   b) Types of cakes
   c) Types of moustaches
   d) Sleeping positions

7. Which is the only organ in the human body that can grow cells in order to regenerate itself?
   a) Brain
   b) Kidney
   c) Liver
   d) Nose

8. Veer Bhoomi is the memorial to which Indian prime minister?
   a) Indira Gandhi
   b) Rajiv Gandhi

c) Pandit Nehru
   d) Lal Bahadur Shastri

9. Mahatma Gandhi once sent an autographed version of what to Henry Ford?
   a) English translation of the *Bhagwad Gita*
   b) A charkha
   c) A khadi shawl
   d) His walking stick

10. In terms of area, which country is more than five times the size of India?
    a) Russia
    b) China
    c) Kazakhstan
    d) Canada

11. If a film is rated 'U', what minimum age would you have to be to watch it in theatres?
    a) No minimum age
    b) Thirteen
    c) Eighteen
    d) Twenty-one

12. In which of these sports is the red card not shown?
    a) Football
    b) Hockey
    c) Table tennis
    d) Billiards

13. All new Euro banknotes feature the name of the currency in Latin, Cyrillic and _____ alphabet.

a) Greek
b) French
c) Arabic
d) Hebrew

14. Which of these is named after the president of a country?
    a) Magsaysay Award
    b) Fields Medal
    c) Pulitzer Prize
    d) Booker Prize

15. The bulk of the silk produced in the world is of which variety?
    a) Eri
    b) Tussar
    c) Mulberry
    d) Muga

BUZZER

1. Strawberries do not have seeds: serious or joking?
2. 'Mannat' is the name of which Hindi film actor's residence?
3. Which Indian award was given to Khan Abdul Ghaffar Khan in 1987 and Nelson Mandela in 1990?
4. How many zeros have to be added to one million to make it ten lakhs?
5. Which mode of transport was once referred to as the 'iron horse': train or submarine?

6. If you are getting a cardiography done, which part of your body will be under examination?
7. *The Pickwick Papers* was the first novel of which author?
8. In Hindu mythology, who is also known as Bajrang Bali?
9. Who became the prime minister of India in 2014?
10. Who was the first of twelve men to walk on the surface of Earth's moon?
11. In the IPL, which colour cap is worn by the highest wicket taker?
12. The Chhatrapati Shivaji Terminus in Mumbai was formally opened on whose golden jubilee?

SET 16

TAKE YOUR PICK

1. Which bird has the lowest body temperature of any bird?
   a) Ostrich
   b) Hummingbird
   c) Kiwi
   d) Penguin

2. Which famous author is credited with popularising expressions like 'foregone conclusion' and 'wild goose chase'?
   a) Lewis Carroll
   b) Thomas Hardy
   c) Charles Dickens
   d) William Shakespeare

3. In 1937, which Indian prime minister wrote an essay in the *Modern Review* of Calcutta under the pen-name Chanakya?
   a) Lal Bahadur Shastri
   b) Indira Gandhi

c) Jawaharlal Nehru
d) P.V. Narasimha Rao

4. Who coined the term radioactivity?
   a) Marie Curie
   b) Henri Becquerel
   c) Alfred Nobel
   d) Ernest Rutherford

5. The black rubber disc puck is used in which sport?
   a) Sepak Takraw
   b) Volleyball
   c) Lacrosse
   d) Ice hockey

6. Which state would you be travelling to if you went through the tourist routes called Beas circuit, Dhauladhar circuit, Sutlej circuit and Tribal circuit?
   a) West Bengal
   b) Himachal Pradesh
   c) Orissa
   d) Rajasthan

7. On which part of the human body would you generally wear a beanie?
   a) Wrist
   b) Head
   c) Ankle
   d) Waist

8. Of all of the portraits painted by Leonardo Da Vinci in Florence, how many survive till date?

a) One
b) Five
c) Twenty
d) None

9. On a standard computer keyboard, the four keys arranged in an inverted T formation have what on them?
   a) Arrows
   b) Dots
   c) Question Marks
   d) Comma

10. What is the name of the witch in the film *Chhota Bheem and the Throne of Bali*?
    a) Indumati
    b) Rangda
    c) Tuntun
    d) Meena

11. Periodontal tissues surround which structure in the human body?
    a) Heart
    b) Teeth
    c) Lungs
    d) Liver

12. Natural teak forests grow in Laos, Myanmar, Thailand and which other country?
    a) China
    b) Sri Lanka
    c) India

d) Japan

13. Which king sent officers known as Dharma Mahamatras to promote dharma throughout his empire?
    a) Ashoka
    b) Samudragupta
    c) Prithviraj Chauhan
    d) Raja Raja Chola

14. Which of these is a percussion instrument?
    a) Sarod
    b) Mridangam
    c) Sarangi
    d) Shehnai

15. The name of which vegetable comes from an Old French word meaning 'head'?
    a) Brinjal
    b) Cabbage
    c) Bottle gourd
    d) Pumpkin

BUZZER

1. More months of the Gregorian calendar have thirty days than thirty-one days: serious or joking?
2. Who is the first sitting US president to have a Twitter account?
3. In which state is the Nagaur Fair held?

4. Sushi is a staple rice dish of the cuisine of which country?
5. In literature, who went to Brobdingnag and Laputa?
6. Which is the world's largest land carnivore: hippopotamus or polar bear?
7. Who is the first cricketer to play in 100 Test victories?
8. Which superhero's real name is Steve Rodgers?
9. The name of which vehicle comes from the Japanese words for 'man-powered carriage'?
10. In the *Ramayana*, Sita grew up in the palace of which king?
11. Who was the director of the 2014 film *Happy New Year*?
12. In 2013, which state achieved the feat of having the lowest dropout rate among school students in India?

SET 17

TAKE YOUR PICK

1. Which superhero was born when Victor Stone met with an accident and his scientist father saved him by replacing over half his body with cybernetic parts?
   a) Cyborg
   b) Iron Man
   c) Hulk
   d) Wolverine

2. Chris Messina, a former designer at Google, proposed which symbol for Twitter that was earlier known as the 'pound symbol'?
   a) Double ticks
   b) Hashtag
   c) At sign
   d) Like

3. Luzon is the largest island of which Asian nation?
   a) The Philippines
   b) Indonesia
   c) Malaysia

d) Japan

4. In which animated film series would you come across a mammoth named Manny, a sabre-tooth tiger named Diego and a sloth named Sid?
   a) *Ice Age*
   b) *Shrek*
   c) *The Lion King*
   d) *Madagascar*

5. The book *Abba–God's Greatest Gift To Us* is about which classical musician of India?
   a) Bismillah Khan
   b) Zakir Hussain
   c) Amjad Ali Khan
   d) Rashid Khan

6. In mid-eighteenth century, the French Commander Bussy made which landmark in Hyderabad his headquarters?
   a) Salar Jung Museum
   b) Golconda Fort
   c) Gol Gumbaz
   d) Charminar

7. Mujibur Rahman was the first prime minister of which country?
   a) Afghanistan
   b) Bangladesh
   c) Sri Lanka
   d) Pakistan

8. Cressida and Desdemona are the moons of which planet?
   a) Uranus
   b) Saturn
   c) Neptune
   d) Jupiter

9. The luxury train Deccan Odyssey is a joint venture between Indian Railways and the government of...
   a) Tamil Nadu
   b) Orissa
   c) Maharashtra
   d) Uttar Pradesh

10. The lower half of the bill of which bird can hold about 11 litres of water, which is more than can be held in its stomach?
    a) Pelican
    b) Crane
    c) Flamingo
    d) Albatross

11. Kufri Chandramukhi, Kufri Jyoti, Kufri Badshah, Kufri Sindhuri, Kufri Lalima are the main varieties of what grown in India?
    a) Wheat
    b) Apple
    c) Potato
    d) Rice

12. Which monument is painted every seven years with approximately 60 tonnes of paint?

a) Qutb Minar
b) Taj Mahal
c) Eiffel Tower
d) Great Wall of China

13. Which Olympic sport takes place on a mat called 'tatami' with the contest lasting five minutes?
    a) Karate
    b) Taekwondo
    c) Judo
    d) Sumo

14. In *Alice's Adventures in Wonderland*, who is the only character whom Alice interacts with outside of Wonderland?
    a) Mad Hatter
    b) Alice's sister
    c) The Queen of Hearts
    d) The Rabbit

15. Which American president gave the White House its official name?
    a) Franklin Roosevelt
    b) Abraham Lincoln
    c) Gerald Ford
    d) Theodore Roosevelt

BUZZER

1. The Bharat Ratna can only be awarded to Indians: serious or joking?

2. Kimigayo is the national anthem of: Japan or Indonesia?
3. *Long Walk to* _____. Fill in the blank to complete the name of Nelson Mandela's autobiography.
4. Which place, famous for its stupas, was known as Kakanaya in ancient times?
5. In the *Mahabharata*, which queen was born to the king of Panchala?
6. Which spice is called zanjabil in Arabic?
7. On 24 January 1950, 284 members appended their signatures to which document?
8. Painted ladies are a species of which insect?
9. Which Indian scientist's first book was *Molecular Diffraction of Light*?
10. Who is the most successful Indian Test captain ever?
11. Which is the second largest state in India in terms of area?
12. What is the source station of the Akal Takht Express?

SET 18

TAKE YOUR PICK

1. With which film did Karan Johar make his directorial debut?
   a) *Kuch Kuch Hota Hai*
   b) *My Name Is Khan*
   c) *Dilwale Dulhania Le Jayenge*
   d) *Student of the Year*

2. Which superhero got his superpowers when he was caught in a gamma bomb explosion while trying to save a teenager's life?
   a) Thor
   b) Hulk
   c) Iron Man
   d) Captain America

3. Which city in Uttarakhand is also known as Mayapuri, Kapila and Gangadwar?
   a) Almora
   b) Haridwar
   c) Dehradun

d) Chamoli

4. Uranus gets its blue-green colour because of the presence of which gas?
   a) Methane
   b) Ammonia
   c) Chlorine
   d) Bromine

5. Kakori kebab, a famous Nawabi preparation, gets its name from a city in…
   a) Andhra Pradesh
   b) West Bengal
   c) Uttar Pradesh
   d) Tamil Nadu

6. International Day of Non Violence is observed on the birth anniversary of which leader?
   a) Vallabhbhai Patel
   b) Jawaharlal Nehru
   c) Mahatma Gandhi
   d) Netaji Subhas Chandra Bose

7. The flag of which of these countries features a yellow sun with a human face known as the Sun of May?
   a) Japan
   b) Argentina
   c) Bangladesh
   d) Brazil

8. Which bird was once known as the 'camel bird' because of its long neck?

a) Pelican
   b) Crane
   c) Ostrich
   d) Albatross

9. Combining Tests, ODIs and T20s, which cricketer has made the most hundreds in his career?
   a) Ricky Ponting
   b) Jacques Kallis
   c) Sachin Tendulkar
   d) Brian Lara

10. Which character from the *Ramayana* was given his name by the devas due to a scar inflicted on his jaw by Indra's vajra?
    a) Hanuman
    b) Indra
    c) Shiva
    d) Brahma

11. In 1946, who designed the cover for Jawaharlal Nehru's book *Discovery of India*?
    a) Bimal Roy
    b) Satyajit Ray
    c) Mrinal Sen
    d) Guru Dutt

12. The four flags planted by Tenzing Norgay and Edmund Hillary on Mount Everest were those of the UK, Nepal, India and the…
    a) United Nations
    b) Greenpeace

c) World Health Organisation
   d) European Union

13. Which computer game features ghosts such as Blinky, Inky, Pinky and Clyde?
    a) Subway Surfers
    b) Temple Run
    c) Candy Crush
    d) Pac-Man

14. Which of these produces insulin and glucagon, two hormones that regulate sugar levels in the blood?
    a) Pancreas
    b) Kidney
    c) Liver
    d) Spleen

15. What is the first line of a song or composition called?
    a) Alaap
    b) Mukhda
    c) Riyaz
    d) Sargam

BUZZER

1. The cerebrum is the largest part of the heart: serious or joking?
2. What do koalas do for 18-22 hours of a day: sleep or eat?
3. The name of which continent means 'opposite to the Arctic'?

4. Hilsa is the national fish of which neighbouring country of India?
5. Who has been the only woman finance minister of India so far?
6. If you arrange the colours of the rainbow in alphabetical order, which colour would be exactly in the middle?
7. The life of which Indian ruler is known mainly through the works of Bana?
8. Which animal appears on the seal of the Reserve Bank of India?
9. In which language did Premchand write *Godaan*?
10. The name of which food item comes from the Greek word makaria?
11. Which term is used when a batsman is out without having faced a single ball?
12. Who is the famous son of actress Neetu Singh?

SET 19

TAKE YOUR PICK

1. Which organisation traces its origin to the Special Police Establishment that was set up in 1941?
   a) CBI
   b) RBI
   c) NCC
   d) BSF

2. In Sanskrit, which tree is referred to as 'kalpa vriksha' as nearly all its parts can be used?
   a) Watermelon
   b) Date
   c) Coconut
   d) Neem

3. The island Más a Tierra on which Alexander Selkirk was marooned, has now officially changed its name to what?
   a) Robinson Crusoe Island
   b) Treasure Island
   c) Captain Nemo Island

d) Gulliver Island

4. Which is the tallest free-standing mountain in the world?
   a) Fuji
   b) Mont Blanc
   c) Kilimanjaro
   d) Aconcagua

5. Which marine creature has more teeth than any other animal?
   a) Dolphin
   b) Jellyfish
   c) Great white shark
   d) Octopus

6. In Harry Potter films, which character has been played by Ralph Fiennes, Christian Coulson and Richard Bremmer?
   a) Lord Voldemort
   b) Vernon Dursley
   c) Albus Dumbledore
   d) Nicolas Flamel

7. In which organ is bile, a greenish-yellow fluid, produced?
   a) Liver
   b) Lungs
   c) Heart
   d) Pancreas

8. Imran Tahir and Usman Khawaja were both born in

Pakistan. Imran plays for South Africa, which team does Usman play for?
a) Australia
b) South Africa
c) West Indies
d) New Zealand

9. The official name of Twitter's bird is …
   a) Sandy
   b) Larry
   c) Jordan
   d) Jack

10. Which spice is called opiumvallmo in Swedish?
    a) Fennel
    b) Poppy seeds
    c) Pepper
    d) Oregano

11. Who was nominated five times for the Nobel Prize in Literature from 1933 to 1937?
    a) S. Radhakrishnan
    b) Zakir Hussain
    c) Lal Bahadur Shastri
    d) Vallabhbhai Patel

12. Which of these elements is named after a country?
    a) Curium
    b) Indium
    c) Francium
    d) Osmium

13. Whose body was enhanced by the modified techno-organic virus, Extremis?
    a) Superman
    b) Spider-Man
    c) Batman
    d) Iron Man

14. The name of which train means 'nonstop' or 'fast' in Bengali?
    a) Rajdhani
    b) Shatabdi
    c) Duronto
    d) Garib Rath

15. The official long name of which country is Hellenic Republic?
    a) Hungary
    b) Spain
    c) Italy
    d) Greece

BUZZER

1. The financial year of India starts in June: serious or joking?
2. Which monument has more steps: Qutb Minar or Charminar?
3. What comes before 'Indians' in the name of an IPL team?
4. Complete this quote by Gandhiji: 'Educate one man,

you educate one person but educate a ____ and you educate a whole civilisation.'
5. A seismograph is an instrument used to detect and record what?
6. Which actor connects *Rowdy Rathore, Thank You and Patiala House*?
7. Which mountain would you be climbing if you set up camp on the Khumbu Glacier?
8. In computers, which sign is called 'aapstert', meaning 'monkey's tail' in South Africa?
9. Which part of the egg contains more protein: the egg white or the yolk?
10. Whose house in Gwalior has become a museum called Sarod Ghar: Amjad Ali Khan or Zakir Hussain?
11. In 1840, what did Rowland Hill describe as 'a bit of paper…back with a glutinous wash'?
12. In which part of the human body would you find the cardiac muscle?

SET 20

TAKE YOUR PICK

1. Which reptile gets its name from the Greek words meaning 'terrible lizard'?
   a) Chameleon
   b) Dinosaur
   c) Tuatara
   d) Snake

2. Kelani Ganga and Kalu Ganga are some of the rivers of which neighbouring country of India?
   a) Nepal
   b) Sri Lanka
   c) Bangladesh
   d) Cambodia

3. Who were the first Indian couple to feature on an Indian postage stamp after Independence?
   a) Kasturba and Mahatma Gandhi
   b) Kamala and Jawaharlal Nehru
   c) Anjali and Sachin Tendulkar
   d) No couple

4. Following the new rules of the ICC, Ajinkya Rahane holds the record of being the last person to do what in international cricket?
   a) Bowl with two hands
   b) Wear a chest guard
   c) Be a runner
   d) Be a captain in his debut Test

5. What are Trinidad Scorpion, Bhut Jolokia, Naga Viper types of?
   a) Snakes
   b) Chillies
   c) Islands
   d) Hats

6. If Hero is Phantom's pet horse, what kind of an animal is Devil?
   a) Lion
   b) Wolf
   c) Camel
   d) Cheetah

7. Which musical instrument is known as clavier in German?
   a) Piano
   b) Trumpet
   c) Mouth Organ
   d) Guitar

8. Which planet was known in ancient Greece by two different names—Phosphorus when it appeared as a morning star and Hesperus when it appeared as an

evening star?
a) Venus
b) Mercury
c) Jupiter
d) Mars

9. Which novel by R.L. Stevenson was first published serially in a children's magazine under the title *The Sea-Cook*?
   a) *Robinson Crusoe*
   b) *Ivanhoe*
   c) *Gulliver's Travels*
   d) *Treasure Island*

10. What does 'L' stand for in the abbreviation ILO?
    a) Legal
    b) Labour
    c) Literary
    d) Livelihood

11. In which state is the Khajuraho Dance Festival held?
    a) Uttar Pradesh
    b) Madhya Pradesh
    c) Rajasthan
    d) Kerala

12. Around 550 AD, Justinian I persuaded two Persian monks from China to smuggle what to Constantinople in the hollows of their bamboo canes?
    a) Tea leaves
    b) Papyrus
    c) Leather shoes

d) Silkworms

13. In the *Mahabharata*, who was the famous son of Hiranya Dhanush, a king of the foresters?
    a) Eklavya
    b) Sudama
    c) Karna
    d) Bharata

14. The antrum and pylorus are the regions of which part of the human body?
    a) Stomach
    b) Gall bladder
    c) Liver
    d) Lungs

15. Which is the only continent without glaciers?
    a) Australia
    b) Antarctica
    c) Europe
    d) Africa

BUZZER

1. Helium is named after the Greek word for hell: serious or joking?
2. The Spanish explorers gave which edible plant product a name meaning 'grinning face'?
3. The first national stamp of Australia featured which animal?

4. The name of which mountain range of the Deccan Plateau means 'seven folds' in Hindi?
5. Who gave his first talk on a religious subject at a deer park in Sarnath?
6. Who is also known as the Bard of Avon?
7. The Karolinska Institute confers which Nobel Prize: medicine, physics or economics?
8. In a dictionary, the name of which month of the year will appear immediately before January?
9. Who was the music director of the 2014 film *Highway*?
10. The name of which member of the UN starts with 'Y'?
11. Contact lenses correct the defects of which sense organ?
12. Which word connects an aromatic plant and a place where money is coined?

ANSWERS

SET 1

TAKE YOUR PICK

1. Kangaroos
2. Rashtrapati Bhavan
3. A camera
4. Earth
5. K.R. Narayanan
6. Brinjal
7. Alexander the Great
8. Sahara
9. Tricolour
10. Olympic flag with five rings; the five colours and white were chosen because they incorporated the colours of all national flags in existence at the time the Olympic flag was created.
11. Pandit Nehru
12. Space bar
13. Kidney
14. C.N.R. Rao

15. Wool; from the Persian word *pašm*.

BUZZER

1. Serious
2. Neck
3. *Kahaani*
4. Green
5. Regional; South Asian Association for Regional Cooperation
6. Mount Fuji
7. Sita
8. Leopard. It means people can't change their basic nature.
9. Three tsps
10. 32. 16 for each team.
11. Vibhushan
12. Afghanistan

SET 2

TAKE YOUR PICK

1. Suresh Raina
2. Ellora Caves
3. Blue ticks
4. Photography
5. Thirty years
6. Shawarma
7. Penguins
8. Rabindranath Tagore

9. Mauritius
10. J
11. Sri Lanka
12. Commissioner
13. Hindi and Urdu
14. Tiger
15. Batik

BUZZER

1. Joking. It is the Hindi name for cinnamon.
2. January
3. Mouth
4. Kohinoor Diamond
5. Jammu
6. *Ramayana*
7. Jawaharlal Nehru; Rajiv Gandhi, the youngest prime minister till date, assumed office at the age of forty-one.
8. Albert Einstein
9. Lahore
10. Ton
11. Table tennis
12. Mountain

SET 3

TAKE YOUR PICK

1. The Vice-President
2. Lucknow

3. Babur
4. Kerala
5. Thomas Alva Edison
6. Bengali
7. Dentist
8. Indian rhinoceros
9. Equals to
10. *A Brief History of Time*. *Wings of Fire* is the autobiography of A.P.J. Abdul Kalam, *Long Walk to Freedom* is the autobiographical work of Nelson Mandela, *The Diary of a Young Girl* is the autobiography of Anne Frank. *A Brief History of Time* is written by Stephen Hawking.
11. Sutlej
12. China
13. Grapes
14. Amitabh Bachchan
15. F1

BUZZER

1. Serious; clams and mussels can also produce pearls.
2. *Twilight*
3. Queen Victoria
4. They weigh the same.
5. April
6. Sherlock Holmes
7. Aravalli Range
8. Statue of Liberty
9. Sleeper
10. Dr Manmohan Singh

11. Neptune
12. Spain

SET 4

TAKE YOUR PICK

1. Retweet
2. Giraffe
3. Panaji
4. Paratha
5. The United States of America
6. Blue card
7. Albert Einstein
8. Barack Obama
9. Perry Mason
10. None
11. Small intestine
12. Humayun's Tomb
13. The Siachen Glacier
14. Paper
15. Buddhism

BUZZER

1. Serious
2. Eye
3. Japan
4. Rice
5. Parachute
6. Grand Trunk Road

7. *Treasure Island*
8. A.P.J. Abdul Kalam. Succeeded by Pratibha Patil.
9. Potato; couch potato.
10. Neptune
11. West Bengal; Darjeeling Zoo.
12. Australia

SET 5

TAKE YOUR PICK

1. Hockey
2. Great white shark
3. WhatsApp
4. Rubber
5. Lakshadweep
6. Veena
7. Mark Antony
8. Pupils
9. Viceroy
10. Godavari
11. Landing on the moon
12. Shortest names of railway stations
13. Poach
14. Exclamation mark
15. White

BUZZER

1. Joking; John Logie Baird did.
2. *Kai Po Che.* Based on the novel *The Three Mistakes of*

My Life by Chetan Bhagat.
3. Omelette; from lemele.
4. Hairstyles
5. Hong Kong
6. Smoke
7. The Mauryas. Mauryan dynasty was between 321–185 BC and the Guptas were from about 320–540 AD.
8. Tamil Nadu
9. Chikankari
10. Sanskrit
11. Cristiano Ronaldo
12. Antarctica

SET 6

TAKE YOUR PICK

1. The Eiffel Tower
2. Africa
3. Ants
4. Chief Justice of India
5. Nepali
6. Coffee pot
7. Namaskar
8. Madhya Pradesh; followed by Arunachal Pradesh at 67,410 square km.
9. Joints
10. Bairam Khan
11. Jakarta
12. Chef
13. Virat Kohli

14. Green
15. Embroidery

BUZZER

1. Serious. Three more storeys were added by his successor and son-in-law, Shams-ud-din Iltutmish.
2. Lewis Caroll; in the book *Alice's Adventures in Wonderland*.
3. Pattachitra paintings
4. Dadasaheb Phalke Award
5. Yolk; from the Old English word geolu.
6. Towel
7. Cube
8. Andaman and Nicobar. The southernmost island is Great Nicobar.
9. Holi
10. Neon
11. Milkha Singh
12. Polar bears

SET 7

TAKE YOUR PICK

1. Skin
2. Cheetah
3. Satyagrahi
4. Chennai Super Kings
5. English (Pirate)
6. Imagination

7. Kathakali
8. Speaker, Lok Sabha
9. *Hamlet*
10. Supreme Court
11. Chola
12. Bhutan
13. Ambulance
14. Alphonso
15. Shift

BUZZER

1. Serious
2. Shahid Kapoor
3. Horse
4. Semolina/Rawa/Suji
5. Germany
6. Star
7. Literature
8. Ajanta Caves
9. Chandragupta Maurya
10. Republic Day
11. Fourteen
12. Protein; from proteios.

SET 8

TAKE YOUR PICK

1. Asiatic lion
2. AC Chair Car

3. Badminton
4. Chlorine
5. A.P.J. Abdul Kalam
6. Rs 1,000
7. Jaundice
8. Tipu Sultan
9. Antarctica
10. Arithmetic
11. Moustaches
12. Amla
13. Start Menu opens
14. Rice
15. Collars

BUZZER

1. Serious
2. India
3. Ben 10
4. June
5. Nepal
6. Gujarat; in the Gir Forest.
7. Napoleon
8. Mandible. The rest are all bones in the leg. The mandible is the jawbone.
9. Maharashtra
10. Moon; from luna; from the belief that changes of the moon caused intermittent insanity.
11. Monitor
12. Dhyan Chand; on 29 August.

SET 9

TAKE YOUR PICK

1. Twelve
2. Horse
3. Low melting point. When a high current flows through the circuit due to overloading or a short circuit, the wires gets heated and melt. As a result, the circuit is broken and current stops flowing.
4. Allahabad
5. Legs
6. Archery
7. Thailand
8. Education
9. Gujarat
10. 1 million
11. Nelson Mandela
12. Ladies' finger
13. Santoor
14. Chikankari
15. Sri Lanka

BUZZER

1. Serious
2. Left
3. Abhishek Bachchan
4. Coffee
5. Nectar
6. Odisha

7. Mughal
8. Brain
9. *Ramayana*
10. Paper
11. Platinum
12. Fiji

SET 10

TAKE YOUR PICK

1. Candela; Candela, unit of luminous intensity, from candle; Hertz, unit of frequency, from the name of H. R. Hertz; Pascal, unit of pressure, after Blaise Pascal; Watt, unit of power, after James Watt.
2. Indian Rhinoceros
3. Rivers
4. Sania Mirza
5. Lal Bahadur Shastri
6. National flag
7. An ostrich egg
8. Gujarat
9. Thirteen
10. Maldives
11. Selfie
12. Coriander
13. Guitar
14. Sarees
15. Netaji Subhas Chandra Bose

BUZZER

1. Joking. It has been shared on four occasions.
2. U
3. Ravi Shankar
4. Kangana Ranaut
5. Bihar
6. Blue
7. Fatehpur Sikri
8. Saturn
9. Swan
10. Oxygen
11. Mumbai Indians
12. Hair

SET 11

TAKE YOUR PICK

1. Indian elephant
2. Allahabad
3. Sixteen
4. Glass bottle
5. Peepal tree
6. Diwali
7. Vitamin C
8. The Statue of Liberty
9. South America
10. Milk
11. Tea bags
12. Odissi

13. Achkan
14. Friday
15. Red

BUZZER

1. Joking; sushi from Japan and pizza from Italy.
2. Po
3. Cricket; from criquer.
4. Interpol (From Inter[national] pol[ice])
5. Gateway of India
6. Tooth
7. Cookie
8. Ganesha. Celebration of Ganesh Chaturthi is usually between 20 August and 15 September every year.
9. Gum
10. Neon; from neos.
11. Taekwondo
12. Karnataka

SET 12

TAKE YOUR PICK

1. Radius
2. Qutb Minar
3. Dhyan Chand Award
4. Chocolate; the Aztecs called chocolate 'xocoatl'.
5. Saturn
6. Potatoes
7. Have tails; apes do not have tails.

8. 22 March
9. Shah Jahan
10. The Corbett National Park
11. Afghanistan
12. Cargos
13. Andaman and Nicobar Islands
14. Spanish
15. Rajkumar Hirani

BUZZER

1. Joking; they are called Vampire bats.
2. Organisation
3. Donald Duck
4. Saffron
5. Nobel Prize
6. Taj Mahal
7. Skin. It is the largest external organ.
8. *Mahabharata*
9. Red
10. Bangladesh
11. Odisha
12. Lucknow

SET 13

TAKE YOUR PICK

1. Greyhound
2. Rashtrapati Bhavan
3. Shooting

4. Orange
5. Land covered with snow
6. Bhoodan
7. Post Offices
8. Blink
9. Florence Nightingale
10. Jammu and Kashmir
11. Weavers
12. Batman
13. Diamond
14. Shoes
15. *Treasure Island*

BUZZER

1. Serious
2. Weblog
3. Jaggu
4. Kiwi
5. Nobel Memorial Prize in Economic Sciences
6. Maharashtra
7. Five
8. Neil Armstrong. 'Neil Armstrong was a hero not just of his time, but of all time,' Barack Obama said via Twitter. 'Thank you, Neil, for showing us the power of one small step.'
9. Sachin Tendulkar
10. Trams
11. Kangaroo
12. Ophelia

SET 14

TAKE YOUR PICK

1. The Eiffel Tower
2. Metal ball
3. Salman Khan
4. Parasite
5. Stomach
6. Mahatma Gandhi
7. Ostrich
8. Dunes
9. Unfriend
10. Crore
11. Temple Run
12. Yellow
13. Bandhni
14. *1984*
15. Fingerprints

BUZZER

1. Joking. It is a kind of fish.
2. Rocket
3. The Great Wall of China
4. A
5. Panipat
6. Lungs
7. Monkey
8. Mother
9. Novak Djokovic

10. Cancellation
11. *Alice's Adventures in Wonderland*
12. White

SET 15

TAKE YOUR PICK

1. Megabyte
2. Giraffe
3. Farhan Akhtar
4. Silver
5. Shiva
6. Sleeping positions
7. Liver
8. Rajiv Gandhi
9. A charkha; the wheel, autographed in Hindi and English, was shipped some 12,000 miles and personally delivered to Ford by T.A. Raman in Greenfield Village, Michigan.
10. Russia
11. No minimum age
12. Billiards
13. Greek
14. Magsaysay Award
15. Mulberry

BUZZER

1. Joking; each strawberry has around 200 seeds.
2. Shah Rukh Khan

3. Bharat Ratna
4. None. 10 lakhs = 1 million.
5. Train
6. Heart
7. Charles Dickens
8. Hanuman
9. Narendra Modi
10. Neil Armstrong
11. Purple
12. Queen Victoria. It was formerly known as the Victoria Terminus.

SET 16

TAKE YOUR PICK

1. Kiwi
2. William Shakespeare. 'fashionable' in *Troilus and Cressida*, 'foregone conclusion' in *Othello* and 'wild goose chase' in *Romeo and Juliet*.
3. Jawaharlal Nehru
4. Marie Curie
5. Ice hockey
6. Himachal Pradesh
7. Head
8. One; Mona Lisa.
9. Arrows. Four arrow keys arranged in an inverted T formation between the typing keys and numeric keypad move the cursor on the screen in small increments.
10. Rangda

11. Teeth
12. India
13. Ashoka
14. Mridangam
15. Cabbage

BUZZER

1. Joking; More months have thirty-one days: January, March, May, July, August, October and December (Seven).
2. Barack Obama
3. Rajasthan
4. Japan
5. Lemuel Gulliver
6. Polar bear
7. Ricky Ponting
8. Captain America
9. Rickshaw
10. Janaka
11. Farah Khan
12. Kerala

SET 17

TAKE YOUR PICK

1. Cyborg
2. Hashtag
3. The Philippines
4. *Ice Age*

5. Amjad Ali Khan
6. Charminar
7. Bangladesh
8. Uranus
9. Maharashtra
10. Pelican
11. Potato
12. Eiffel Tower
13. Judo. Developed from jujitsu, the hand-to-hand combat technique of ancient samurai warriors, judo basically involves throwing opponents to the floor and holding them in submission.
14. Alice's sister
15. Theodore Roosevelt

BUZZER

1. Joking
2. Japan
3. Freedom
4. Sanchi
5. Draupadi
6. Ginger
7. The Constitution of India. It was adopted on 26 November 1949, and came into force on 26 January 1950.
8. Butterfly
9. C.V. Raman
10. M.S. Dhoni. He crossed Sourav Ganguly's record of twenty-one Test wins to become the most successful Test captain for India.

11. Madhya Pradesh
12. Amritsar

SET 18

TAKE YOUR PICK

1. *Kuch Kuch Hota Hai*
2. Hulk
3. Haridwar
4. Methane
5. Uttar Pradesh
6. Mahatma Gandhi
7. Argentina
8. Ostrich. Also because of its prominent eyes, and sweeping eyelashes, as well as its jolting walk.
9. Sachin Tendulkar
10. Hanuman. Hanu-jawbone or chin.
11. Satyajit Ray
12. United Nations
13. Pac-Man. Creator Toru Iwatani, based on a pizza with a slice missing.
14. Pancreas
15. Mukhda

BUZZER

1. Joking. The Brain.
2. Sleep
3. The continent of Antarctica
4. Bangladesh

5. Indira Gandhi; for a year from 1970 to 1971.
6. Orange
7. Harshavardhana
8. Tiger
9. Hindi
10. Macaroni
11. Diamond Duck
12. Ranbir Kapoor

SET 19

TAKE YOUR PICK

1. CBI (Central Bureau of Investigation)
2. Coconut
3. Robinson Crusoe Island
4. Kilimanjaro
5. Dolphin. Some dolphins have over 200 teeth.
6. Lord Voldemort
7. Liver
8. Australia
9. Larry
10. Poppy seeds
11. S. Radhakrishnan
12. Francium
13. Iron Man
14. Duronto
15. Greece

BUZZER

1. Joking. It starts in April.
2. Qutb Minar. 379 steps.
3. Mumbai
4. Woman
5. Earthquake
6. Akshay Kumar
7. Mount Everest
8. At the rate of or @
9. Egg white
10. Amjad Ali Khan
11. Stamp
12. Heart

SET 20

TAKE YOUR PICK

1. Dinosaur; from Greek deinos (terrible)+sauros (lizard).
2. Sri Lanka
3. Kasturba and Mahatma Gandhi
4. Be a runner. For Parthiv Patel during the 4th ODI between India and England at Lord's in September 2011.
5. Chillies. Some of the hottest chillies in the world
6. Wolf
7. Piano
8. Venus
9. *Treasure Island*

10. Labour
11. Madhya Pradesh
12. Silkworms
13. Eklavya
14. Stomach
15. Australia

BUZZER

1. Joking. It is named after the Greek word for the sun.
2. Coconut
3. Kangaroo
4. Satpura Range
5. Buddha
6. William Shakespeare
7. Medicine
8. February
9. A.R. Rahman
10. Yemen
11. Eyes
12. Mint

www.ingramcontent.com/pod-product-compliance
Lightning Source LLC
Chambersburg PA
CBHW032001080426
42735CB00007B/472